DISCOVERING
EARTHQUAKES

Mysteries • Secret Codes • Games • Mazes

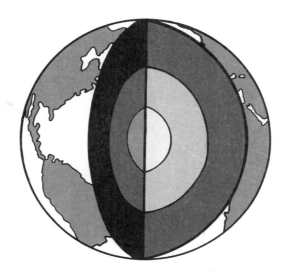

Nancy Field
Adele Schepige

Illustrated by Nancy Lynch

Text copyright © 1995 Dog-Eared Publications
Artwork copyright © 1995 Nancy Lynch

Third Printing 2002

ISBN 0-941042-12-X

 Printed in the USA on
Recycled Paper with Soy Ink

Earthquakes Happen More

Where can you go to be absolutely safe from earthquakes? Nowhere on this earth!

Every year, nearly half a million earthquakes shake and rumble in some part of our planet. An earthquake can happen almost anywhere. Every state and province of North America may experience an earthquake.

What is going on?

Earthquakes are natural. Just like volcanoes, hurricanes, tornadoes, and fires, they help shape our everchanging earth.

Let's learn more about what really happens where there is an earthquake. Let's ask these scientists.

"Most earthquakes are very small," the scientists tell us. "Some are large enough to damage buildings. A few huge ones wipe out entire towns or cities."

"I don't like them," you say.

"I wish earthquakes wouldn't happen at all."

"The world would be a nicer place with no natural disasters," the scientist answers. "But if we learn about earthquakes, we may be able to predict when and where they'll happen next time. Best of all, we can find ways to keep people safer."

Your *Discovering Earthquakes* book will help you learn more about earthquakes. You'll even learn what YOU can do to keep people safer.

What kind of damage can happen?
See page 28

Can we predict future earthquakes?
See page 34

How can I stay safe during an earthquake?
See page 27

How can we protect our community?
Play the game on pages 20 to 23

What can we learn about earthquakes that happened long ago?
Solve the mystery on page 32

Often Than You Think!

A long time ago, people thought

…earthquakes were mysteries. They made up stories, called myths, to help explain these strange happenings.

Here are several myths from around the world. **Draw a line from each story to the place where the myth started**.

2. According to the Mayans of Central America, the earth was a cube. Each corner was held up by gods called the Vashakmen. Whenever the Vashakmen decided the world was over populated, they would tip it to get rid of some people. The tipping caused an earthquake.

1. Reelfoot Lake, Tennessee, was named after a Chickasaw Indian chief who had a club foot. The chief stole a princess from the Choctaw Indian tribe to take as his wife. He dreamed the earth would tremble in rage. During the wedding, the ground shook. The Mississippi River gathered its waters and flowed backward over the town. Everyone drowned.

3. Native Americans from the San Gabriel Valley of California thought the Great Spirit built the earth on the shells of six turtles. The animals were told not to move. When they argued, the turtles began to swim apart. This caused an earthquake. Because the earth was so heavy, the turtles had to stop moving. They also had to stop fighting.

4. In Scandinavia, the god Loki killed his brother. As punishment, he was tied to a rock. A snake slowly dropped poison on Loki's upturned face, but Loki's wife caught the poison in a dish. Whenever she emptied the dish, some poison fell on Loki's head. He shook and so did the earth.

9. One Chinese legend said the earth rested on an ox. The ox usually gave the earth a smooth ride. When the ox switched the earth from shoulder to shoulder, the earth would quake.

10. Ancient Japanese thought their islands rested on the back of a giant catfish that lived in the mud under the sea. A god called Kashima kept the catfish from pulling pranks. Whenever Kashima lost control, the catfish would thrash about and cause the earth to shake.

8. People from West Africa thought the earth was a flat disk, held up on one side by an enormous mountain and the other by a giant. The giant's wife held up the sky. The earth trembled whenever he decided to hug her.

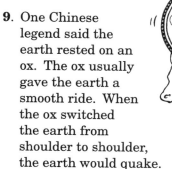

7. The lamas, or Buddhist priests, of Mongolia thought the world sat on the back of an immense frog. If the frog moved its feet or head, there was an earthquake.

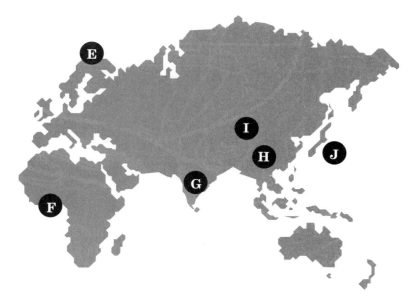

5. The Tlingit Indians of Alaska believed a demon who lived in an underwater cavern wanted to change strangers into tame bears. When the furious demon tried to capture the people, he would stir up the land and water. This caused the earthquakes.

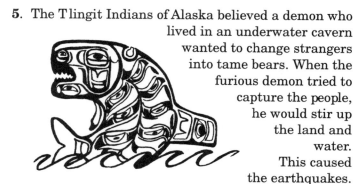

6. In India, the Hindus told of four elephants holding up the earth. These animals stood on the back of a turtle. The turtle stood on the back of a cobra. If any of the animals moved, there was an earthquake.

Use your imagination. Write your own story and draw a picture about what causes earthquakes.

Answers on last page

Solving the Mystery

Today we don't have to rely on myths. We have scientists, called **seismologists**, who study earthquakes. They have learned much about the inside and the outside of the earth. It is easier to study the outside of the earth. We live on it and can see it. How do you suppose you might study the inside?

Imagine you are given a present. You don't open it right away. Instead, you try to guess what is in the box. How would you get clues to help you figure out what the present is? Finish the list for the child below.

Ideas for Clues

1. Shake the box

2.

3.

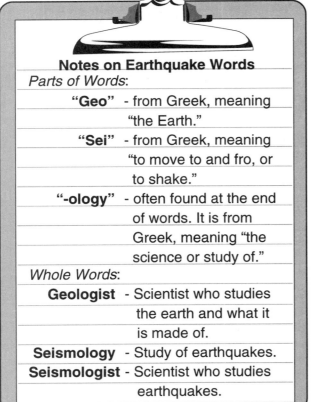

Notes on Earthquake Words

Parts of Words:

"Geo" - from Greek, meaning "the Earth."

"Sei" - from Greek, meaning "to move to and fro, or to shake."

"-ology" - often found at the end of words. It is from Greek, meaning "the science or study of."

Whole Words:

Geologist - Scientist who studies the earth and what it is made of.

Seismology - Study of earthquakes.

Seismologist - Scientist who studies earthquakes.

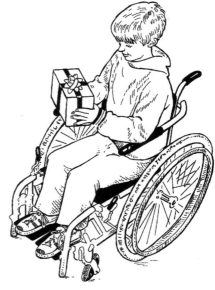

Scientists do the same thing when they study the inside of the earth. They use clues from scientific studies of the energy generated by the earthquake to tell them what the earth's inside is like.

The Inside Story

The earth's interior is arranged in layers like an egg, with a shell, a white and a yolk.

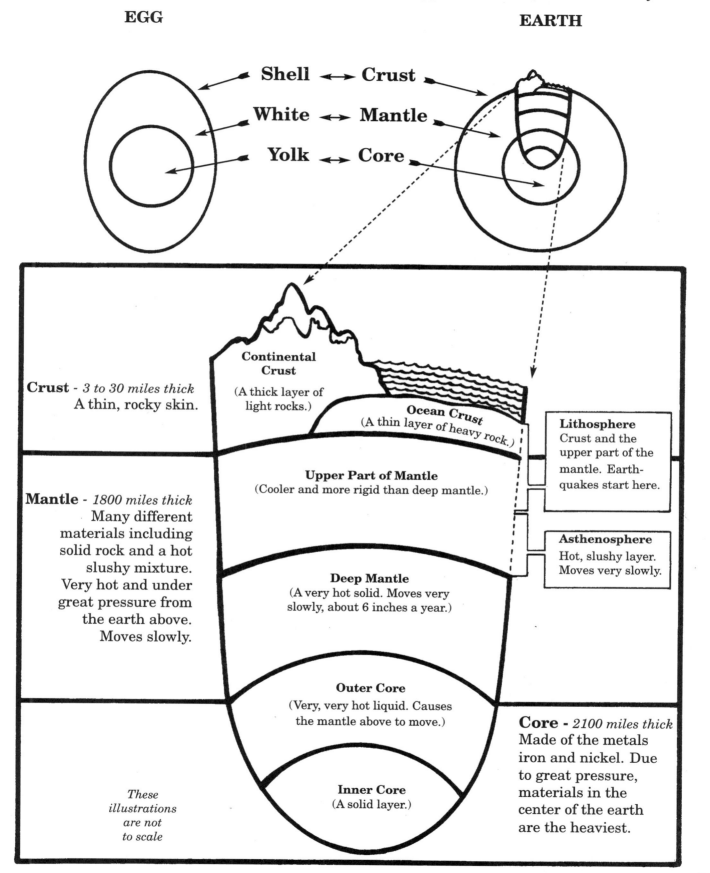

EGG

EARTH

Shell ⟷ Crust

White ⟷ Mantle

Yolk ⟷ Core

Crust - *3 to 30 miles thick*
A thin, rocky skin.

Continental Crust
(A thick layer of light rocks.)

Ocean Crust
(A thin layer of heavy rock.)

Lithosphere
Crust and the upper part of the mantle. Earthquakes start here.

Mantle - *1800 miles thick*
Many different materials including solid rock and a hot slushy mixture. Very hot and under great pressure from the earth above. Moves slowly.

Upper Part of Mantle
(Cooler and more rigid than deep mantle.)

Asthenosphere
Hot, slushy layer. Moves very slowly.

Deep Mantle
(A very hot solid. Moves very slowly, about 6 inches a year.)

Outer Core
(Very, very hot liquid. Causes the mantle above to move.)

These illustrations are not to scale

Inner Core
(A solid layer.)

Core - *2100 miles thick*
Made of the metals iron and nickel. Due to great pressure, materials in the center of the earth are the heaviest.

A Closer Look

Let's look at the crust and the upper part of the mantle (lithosphere). Our earth's mantle is cracked into about 20 plates. The cracks look like cracks in a broken eggshell.

Seven of these plates are large ones. The plates form the land we stand on, our continents, and our ocean floor. They float and move like rafts on top of the mantle.

What causes the plates to move? Here are some imaginary explorers who live under the earth's crust. Let's call them terranauts. "Terra" means "earth." "Naut" means "sailor." These little folks can help explain how earthquakes and volcanoes can be related. Some of the forces that cause earthquakes also produce volcanoes.

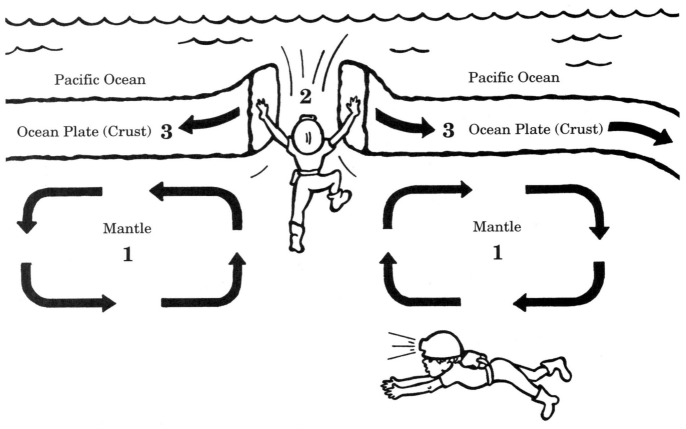

1. The hottest parts of the mantle rise to the top, move across the surface, cool, and sink back down to the bottom. Boiling water does the same thing. The mantle material flows about as fast as your fingernail grows.

2. In some places the mantle becomes so hot it melts to form molten rock called **magma**. Sometimes magma rises up through the breaks in the ocean's crust.

3. As magma rises, it cools to make new ocean crust. That new crust pushes the old crust out of the way, in opposite directions. This force is called "ridge push."

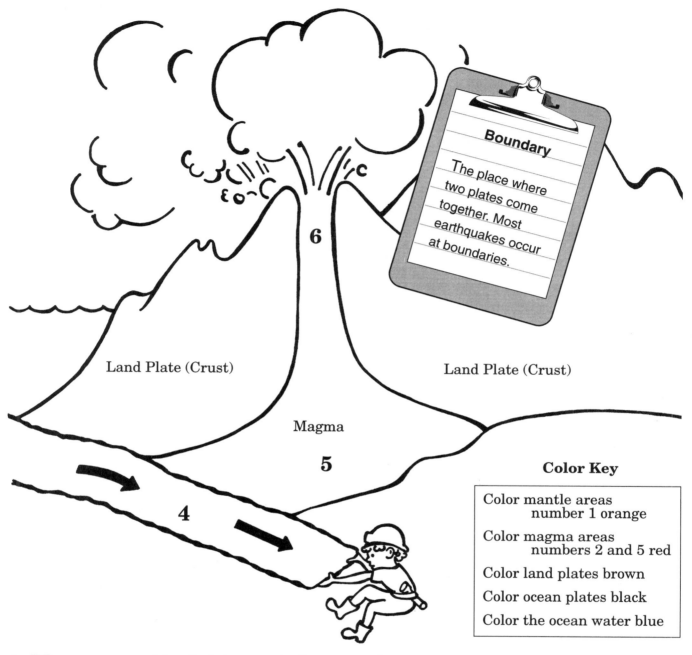

Land Plate (Crust)

Land Plate (Crust)

Magma

Boundary

The place where two plates come together. Most earthquakes occur at boundaries.

Color Key

Color mantle areas
 number 1 orange

Color magma areas
 numbers 2 and 5 red

Color land plates brown

Color ocean plates black

Color the ocean water blue

4. Where ocean and land plates meet, the ocean plates can push under the land plates. This is called **subduction**. However, the ocean plate does not slide smoothly under the land plate. Pushing and rubbing causes **earthquakes**.

5. With increasing pressure and depth, the oceanic plate becomes hotter. Some of it melts and forms magma.

6. Magma finds its way to weak spots in the earth's crust and breaks through to form a volcano. Magma moving below the earth's surface also causes earthquakes.

This scientist's understanding, or **theory**, of how the plates move is called **plate tectonics**. This theory helps explain why volcanoes and earthquakes occur where they do.

All Cracked Up

Each plate has a name. Most of the names come from the ocean or continent which is part of the plate. See if you can guess the plate's name. **Then, use the secret code to help you label the plates and learn their names**.

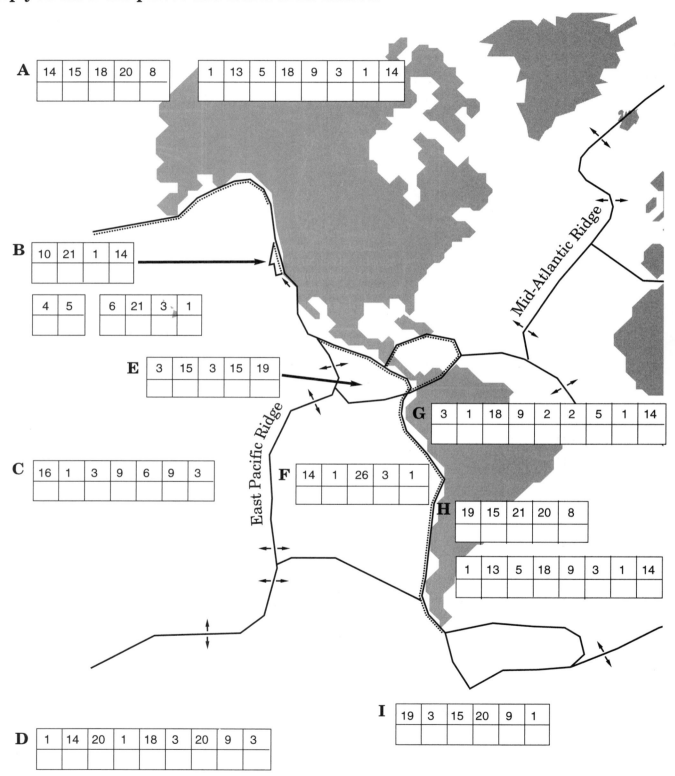

A

14	15	18	20	8

1	13	5	18	9	3	1	14

B

10	21	1	14

4	5

6	21	3	1

E

3	15	3	15	19

G

3	1	18	9	2	2	5	1	14

C

16	1	3	9	6	9	3

F

14	1	26	3	1

H

19	15	21	20	8

1	13	5	18	9	3	1	14

I

19	3	15	20	9	1

D

1	14	20	1	18	3	20	9	3

Notice the way the small arrows point on the map. They tell you which way the plates are moving. This symbol ·········· means one plate is being pushed under the other. This is a subduction zone.

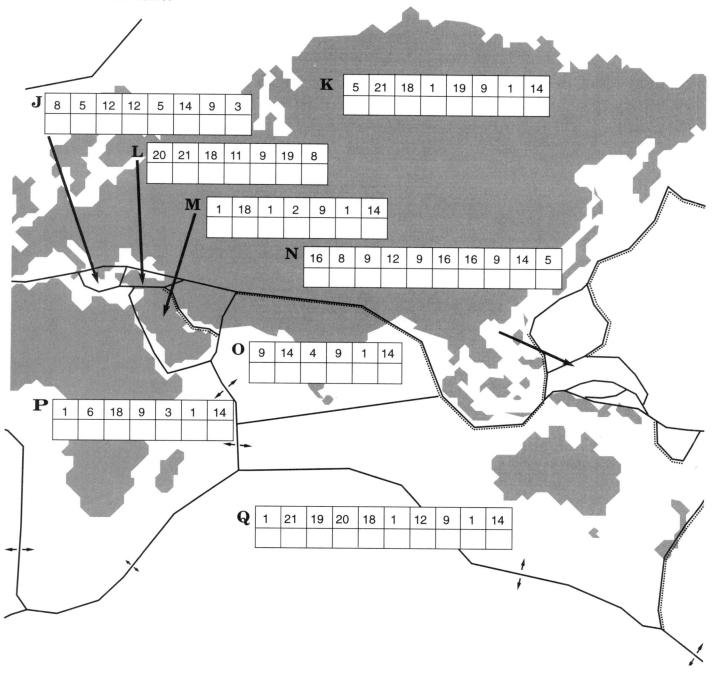

K	5	21	18	1	19	9	1	14	

J	8	5	12	12	5	14	9	3

L	20	21	18	11	9	19	8

M	1	18	1	2	9	1	14

N	16	8	9	12	9	16	16	9	14	5

O	9	14	4	9	1	14

P	1	6	18	9	3	1	14

Q	1	21	19	20	18	1	12	9	1	14

SECRET CODE:

1	2	3	4	5	6	7	8	9	10	11	12	13	14	15	16	17	18	19	20	21	22	23	24	25	26
A	B	C	D	E	F	G	H	I	J	K	L	M	N	O	P	Q	R	S	T	U	V	W	X	Y	Z

Answers on last page

Plates on the Move

Most earthquakes occur along plate boundaries. It is possible for the plates to move quickly, several feet or meters at a time. But most of the time, the plates move slowly, just a few inches or centimeters each year.

How the plates move in relation to each other determines what happens to the crust. Major and minor earthquakes can occur during these plate movements.

Plates can move toward each other or collide. Scientists say they **converge**.

Plate   Fault

Plates can move apart. Scientists say they **diverge**.

What is a Fault?

A **fault** is a crack in the earth's crust where movement has occurred. Rock on one side of a fault may move up, down, or sideways in relation to the rock on the other side. Many faults are at plate boundaries. But there are plenty of faults other places too. Scientists are now searching for faults deep in the earth.

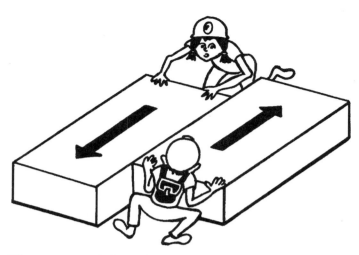

Plates can slide sideways past each other.
Scientists call this **lateral** or **transform plate movement**.

When the edges of the plates get caught or snagged, stress builds up. When the strain becomes too great, the plates suddenly move to a new position. This causes an earthquake. The earthquake relieves the stress for a while.

Famous Fault

What is the most famous fault in North America? Some would say it is the San Andreas Fault in California. It is a transform fault. What kind of movement does this fault have?

It stretches over 600 miles (950 kilometers) from San Francisco to Mexico. Many earthquakes occur along this fault. It is an active fault. and has been active over a very long time.

The Pacific Plate is sliding slightly faster than the North American Plate. Many scientists believe that some day Los Angeles and San Francisco will become next door neighbors. If the Pacific Plate is moving north about 2 inches faster a year than the North American Plate, how long will it take for Los Angeles to be next to San Francisco? The two cities are now about 350 miles (580 kilometers) apart.

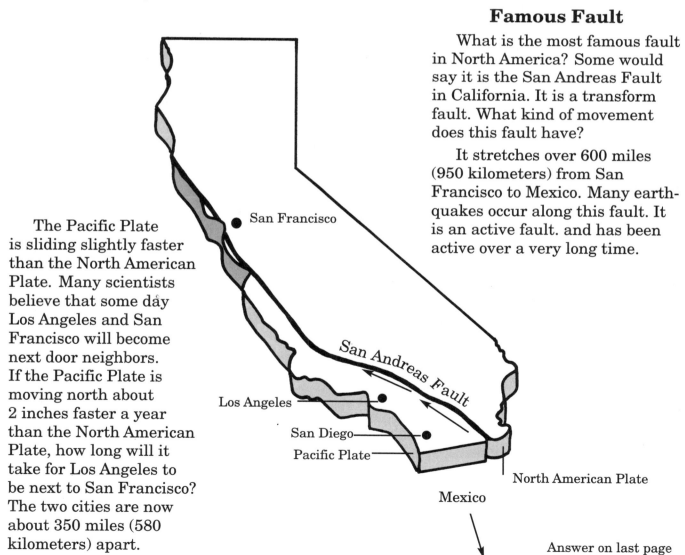

San Francisco

San Andreas Fault

Los Angeles
San Diego
Pacific Plate
North American Plate
Mexico

Answer on last page

Stretch and Snap

What happens to the earth when an earthquake occurs? The rocks in the earth change almost like a breaking stick. If you have ever tried to break a stick, you know that some are easier to break than others.

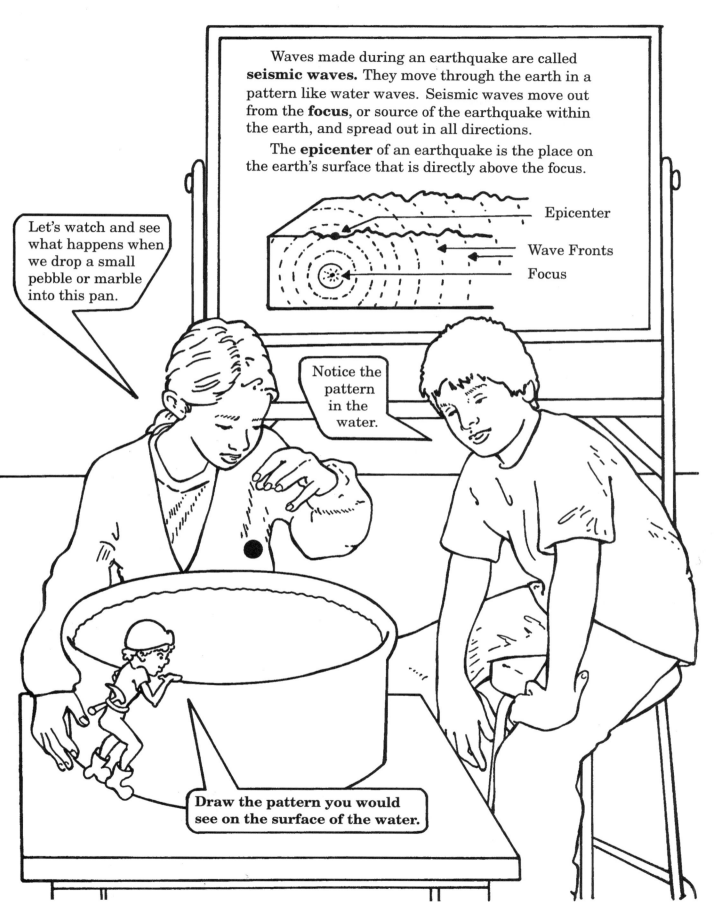

Seismologist's Lab

A seismograph detects and records earthquake waves. There are thousands of seismographs all over the earth. Each one makes a drawing of lines on paper that is called a seismogram. Seismograms show that there are two main kinds of waves: **seismic** or **body waves** and **surface waves**. P and S waves are types of seismic waves. By studying the seismograms from at least three different seismograph stations, a scientist can locate the epicenter of an earthquake.

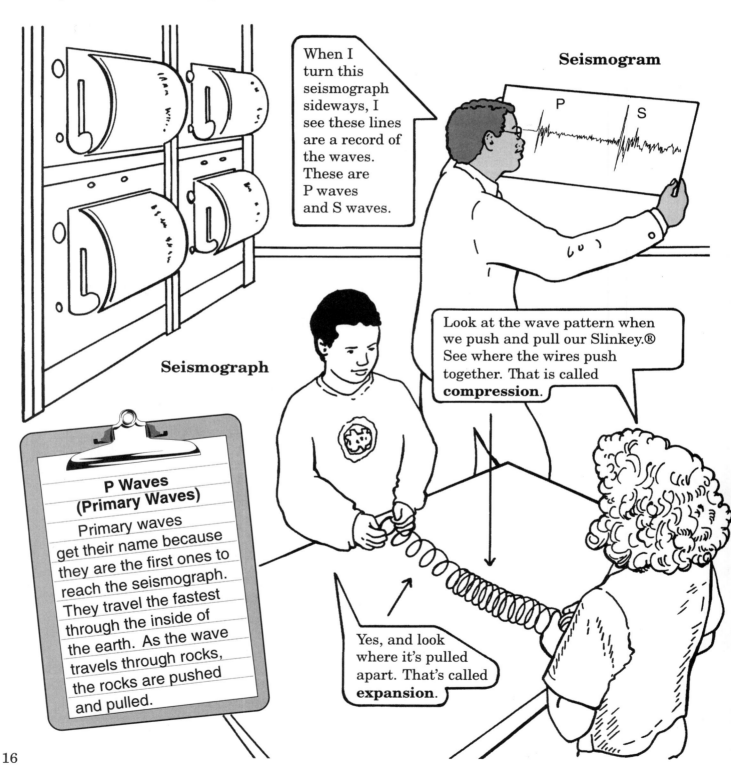

When I turn this seismograph sideways, I see these lines are a record of the waves. These are P waves and S waves.

Seismogram

P   S

Look at the wave pattern when we push and pull our Slinkey.® See where the wires push together. That is called **compression**.

Seismograph

P Waves (Primary Waves)

Primary waves get their name because they are the first ones to reach the seismograph. They travel the fastest through the inside of the earth. As the wave travels through rocks, the rocks are pushed and pulled.

Yes, and look where it's pulled apart. That's called **expansion**.

S Waves
(Secondary Waves)

Secondary waves are the second ones to reach the seismograph station. S waves do not push and pull like a Slinkey® when they travel through the earth. They move the way a rope moves. They cause earth materials to move up and down or side to side.

To see the motion of S waves, we'll need a rope. Let's tie one end of the rope to something that doesn't move. Watch how the rope moves when I flip it up and down.

Now, I'll try it side to side. This must be another way an S wave moves through the earth.

Surface Waves

Surface waves are the last waves to reach the seismograph. They only travel along the earth's surface. Surface waves move up and down like ocean waves. They also move side to side the way a snake moves. Their up-and-down and side-to-side motion is what causes most of the damage, trembling and shaking during earthquakes. They are the reason we seem to feel the earth move under our feet.

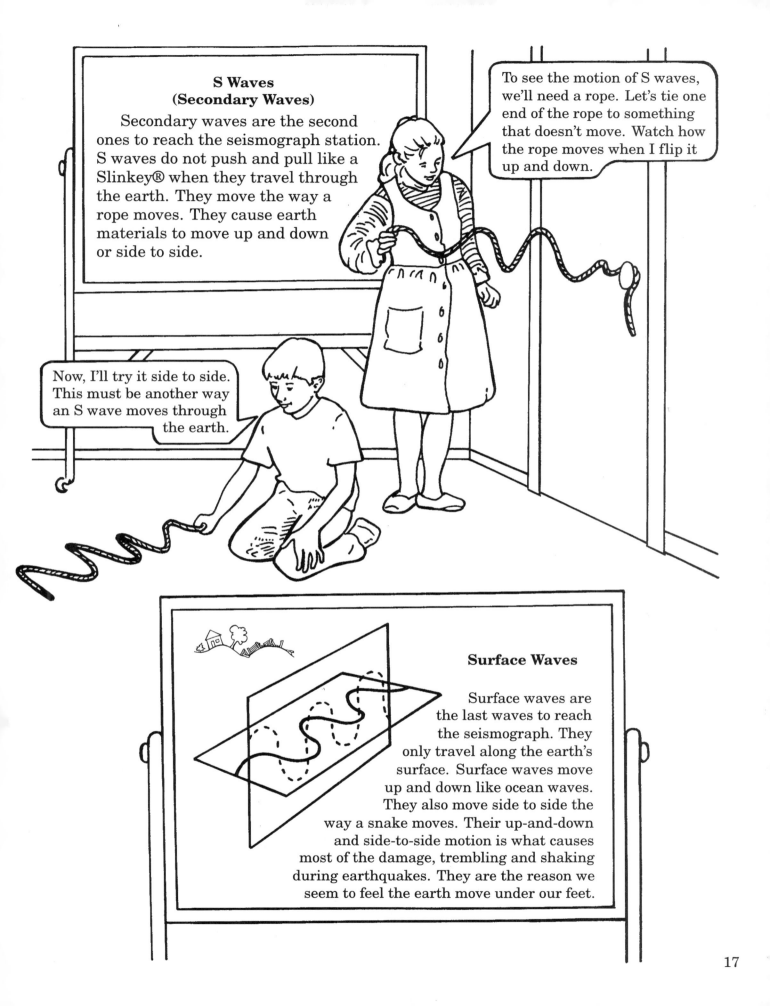

How Big Was It?

Scientists use two different scales for measuring the strength of an earthquake: the **Mercalli Scale** and the **Richter Scale**.

The Mercalli Scale uses Roman numerals to describe effects of earthquakes. It is based on how much damage is caused. **Put the pictures within the columns below in order**. Write a Roman numeral from I to XII by each picture, with I being the least damage and XII the most damage.

Mercalli Scale

Number this column from I to IV.

A _____ Felt by some people. Hanging objects may swing.

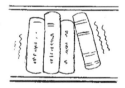

B _____ Felt indoors. Vibration is like that caused by a passing truck.

C _____ Hardly felt by people. Detected by instruments.

D _____ Felt by many indoors and a few outdoors. At night some wake up. Dishes, windows and doors rattle.

Number this column from V to VIII.

E _____ Most are alarmed and run outside. Well constructed buildings are damaged a little, and poorly constructed buildings are hurt more.

F _____ Specially designed structures show little damage. Ordinary ones show more damage. Poorly built structures show great damage.

G _____ Felt by nearly all. Many wake up. Some dishes and windows break. Unstable objects overturn.

H _____ Felt by all. Many are frightened and run outdoors. Some heavy furniture moves. Some plaster falls.

Number this column from IX to XII.

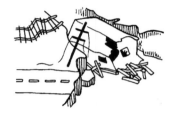

I _____ Almost all buildings and bridges are destroyed. Railroad tracks bend. Broad cracks appear in the ground.

J _____ All buildings are damaged. Some buildings collapse. Underground pipes break.

K _____ Total destruction. Waves show up on the ground surface.

L _____ Many buildings are destroyed. Ground cracks apart. Landslides occur on steep slopes.

UPDATE

Since this book was published, earthquake science continues to grow. Today, earthquakes may be reported to have magnitudes of less than 1.0 and more than 9.0 on the Richter Scale. An earthquake with magnitude equal to 1 is a weak quake. One with magnitude 9.0 is a very strong quake. The Alaskan earthquake of 1964 is recorded as having been a 9.2. A 1960 quake in Chile is recorded as a 9.5.

Many newspapers still report the magnitude of an earth quake using the Richter Scale. However, because of new technology, the US Geological Survey and most international seismologists are now using a **Moment Magnitude** scale to describe the size of earthquakes. This is considered the most accurate way to measure the big earthquakes, as it is based on the amount of energy released by the quake.

The Richter scale measures only the high-frequency waves that travel through the body of the rock. These waves are most damaging to small structures, like homes to buildings a few stories tall.

But the bigger the earthquake, the more long, slow waves it produces. This turns out to be a key difference between larger and smaller earthquakes—the big ones shake the ground much longer. They put out more long, slow swells of the type that can damage very tall buildings and bridges.

New seismic instruments can now capture all types of waves, both the high frequency and the long, slow waves. These waves contain information on the "moment" of the earthquake—which is proportional to the energy released in the event. The information from the seismogram is used to determine the "Moment Magnitude" which applies to the very smallest through the very largest earthquakes.

Richter Scale

Scientists began using the Richter Scale in 1935. It is named after the scientist Charles Richter. A number is used to represent the total amount of energy released, or the **magnitude**, of the quake. On the Richter Scale, an earthquake with magnitude equal to 1 is the weakest quake. One with magnitude 9.0 is the strongest. No earthquake has ever been recorded as high as a 9.0. A higher number on the scale means more energy has been released, and the waves are bigger.

Because there is so much variation in strength, the scale is divided into smaller parts (more precise numbers). For example, the 1993 Oregon earthquake was up to 5.7.

	Magnitude on Richter Scale	*Relative Energy Release*
WEAK — Feels like the rumblings of a passing train.	1, 2	1
	3	30
Equal to the energy of 1000 tons of explosives.	4	900
MODERATE	5	
STRONG	6	
MAJOR	7	
GREAT — Equal to the energy of 200 one-megaton nuclear bombs.	8, 9	

Let's compare an earthquake with a magnitude 1 with others on the Richter Scale. A magnitude 2 releases 30 times more energy. Each increase in magnitude of 1 unit equals an increase of about 30 times the energy released. This is called a "relative scale" because everything is compared to magnitude 1. This increase in energy from one level of the Richter Scale to the next may be difficult to picture. For comparison, think of how the weight of larger animals compares to a guinea pig of one pound.

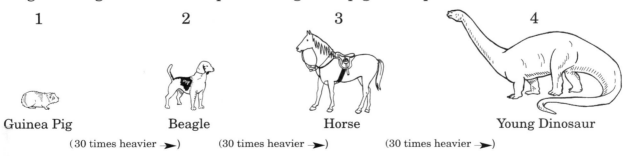

1 Guinea Pig   2 Beagle   3 Horse   4 Young Dinosaur

(30 times heavier ➤)   (30 times heavier ➤)   (30 times heavier ➤)

On the pyramid above, figure out the relative energy released for each magnitude of the Richter Scale. The first three are done for you.

Answers on last page

Safe or Unsafe?

Compare the two rooms on this page. How are they different? Which one is safer and why? What are the dangers in the other picture?

Answers on last page

Earthquake Safety Cop

All communities need to be prepared for an earthquake. Help your community decide if it is ready. As an Earthquake Safety Cop, it is your job to visit different places. Find out if there are hazards and help fix them. A hazard is anything or any condition that might cause damage. Because it is important for the community to work together, all the people playing the game will be a team. Knowing what to do is everyone's best protection. You are all responsible for your community's future safety.

Object: Collect enough points to show that your community has passed the safety test.

You will need:

- Six objects (paper or pebbles) numbered 1, 2, 3, 4, 5 and 6, in a container. You might also use die.

- A playing piece – Each player needs to make his or her own playing piece. It could be a pebble or coin, or you can trace one of these patterns. Cut out the pattern, and tape a penny to the back.

Directions:

1. Place your playing piece at START. Draw a number to see who goes first.
2. When it is your turn, draw a number and move the correct number of squares. Follow the instructions on the board.
3. This is a community center symbol .... ©
   You are invited by the mayor of the city to join a committee. When you land on one of these spaces, stay here, but draw another number to see what happens at the community center.
4. Keep track of your points. At the end, all players total your points. Use the chart below to find out if your community is ready for an earthquake.

Number of Players	Outstanding	Community passes, but needs improvement	Not Prepared
	The community is prepared.	Keep the points. Play a little longer to see if preparedness improves.	Either play again now, or store your points and play again another time.
1	400	201	200 or less
2	700	*501	500 or less
3	1000	801	800 or less
4	1300	1101	1100 or less
5	1600	1401	1400 or less
6	1900	1701	1700 or less
More	Add 300 points for each	Add 300 points for each	Add 300 points for each

For more information contact your local emergency management or civil defense office and your local Red Cross chapter.

21

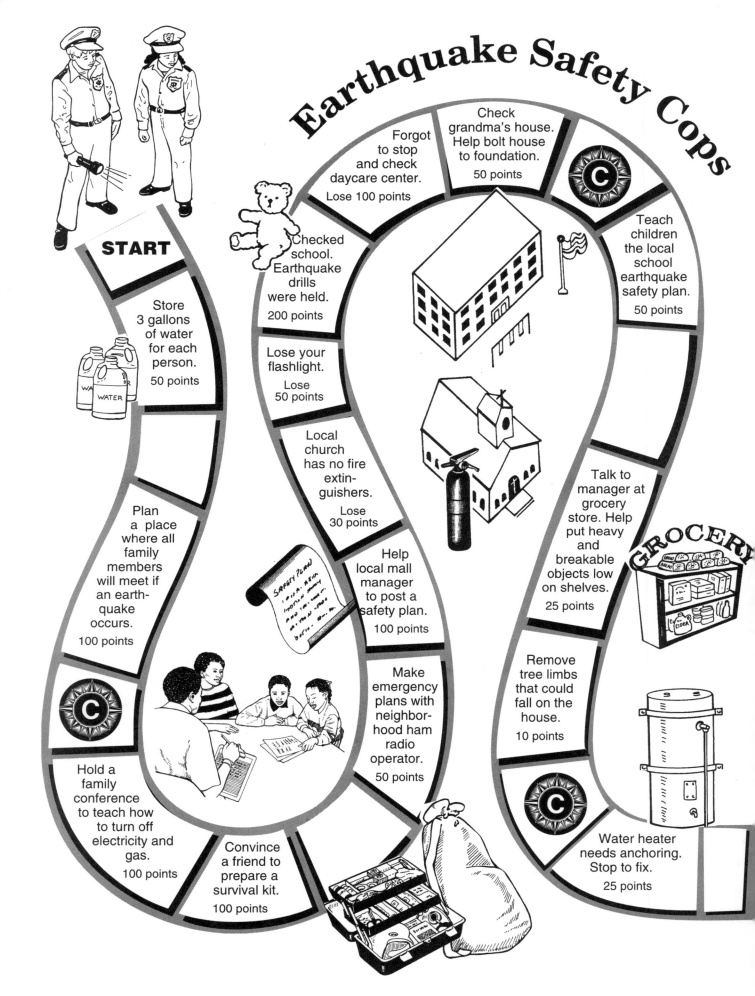

Earthquake Safety Cops

START

Store 3 gallons of water for each person. 50 points

Plan a place where all family members will meet if an earthquake occurs. 100 points

C

Hold a family conference to teach how to turn off electricity and gas. 100 points

Convince a friend to prepare a survival kit. 100 points

Make emergency plans with neighborhood ham radio operator. 50 points

Help local mall manager to post a safety plan. 100 points

Local church has no fire extinguishers. Lose 30 points

Lose your flashlight. Lose 50 points

Checked school. Earthquake drills were held. 200 points

Forgot to stop and check daycare center. Lose 100 points

Check grandma's house. Help bolt house to foundation. 50 points

C

Teach children the local school earthquake safety plan. 50 points

Talk to manager at grocery store. Help put heavy and breakable objects low on shelves. 25 points

GROCERY

Remove tree limbs that could fall on the house. 10 points

C

Water heater needs anchoring. Stop to fix. 25 points

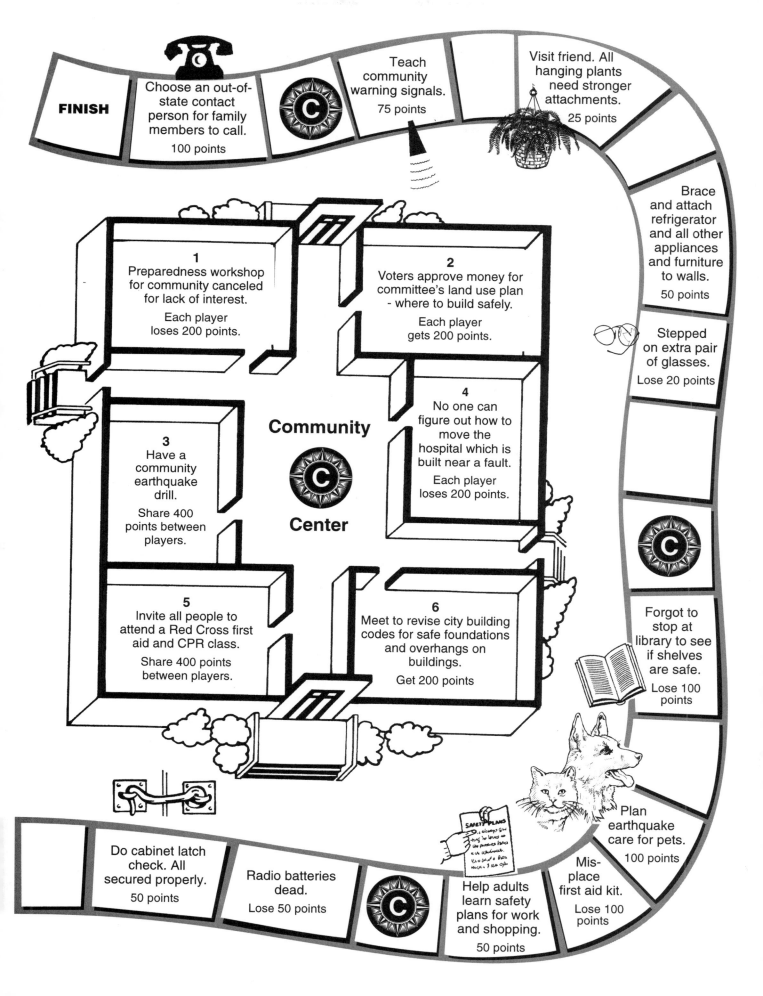

FINISH

Choose an out-of-state contact person for family members to call.
100 points

Teach community warning signals.
75 points

Visit friend. All hanging plants need stronger attachments.
25 points

Brace and attach refrigerator and all other appliances and furniture to walls.
50 points

Stepped on extra pair of glasses.
Lose 20 points

Forgot to stop at library to see if shelves are safe.
Lose 100 points

Plan earthquake care for pets.
100 points

Mis-place first aid kit.
Lose 100 points

Help adults learn safety plans for work and shopping.
50 points

Radio batteries dead.
Lose 50 points

Do cabinet latch check. All secured properly.
50 points

Community

C

Center

1
Preparedness workshop for community canceled for lack of interest.
Each player loses 200 points.

2
Voters approve money for committee's land use plan - where to build safely.
Each player gets 200 points.

3
Have a community earthquake drill.
Share 400 points between players.

4
No one can figure out how to move the hospital which is built near a fault.
Each player loses 200 points.

5
Invite all people to attend a Red Cross first aid and CPR class.
Share 400 points between players.

6
Meet to revise city building codes for safe foundations and overhangs on buildings.
Get 200 points

How Can We Make Buildings Safe?

Earthquakes usually don't kill people: damaged structures kill people. When the ground moves buildings rock, sway and absorb the motion. If they don't, they can be damaged or destroyed. Years ago, no one knew how to make structures resistant to earthquakes. Nowadays, new buildings in earthquake zones are usually made as safe as possible. When the ground moves, the buildings can move up and down or back and forth, without being ruined. No building is completely earthquake-proof, but it can be earthquake resistant. How can we make homes and buildings safer?

Construction Material

Soil Liquefaction

Part of Mexico City is built on the soft soil of an ancient lake bed. When seismic waves come through here, the soil wobbles like Jell-O.® This is called **soil liquefaction**. In 1985, an earthquake that registered 8.1 on the Richter Scale struck Mexico City. Even though the epicenter was 400 miles away, 250 buildings collapsed and thousands of others were damaged in Mexico City.

Old brick or cement houses, not reinforced by steel, can collapse in earthquakes.

Soft Soil

Rock

A well built wood frame house is one of the safest shelters. The frame is like the skeleton of the house. Wood frames are a little bendable.

Building Site

Rock is a safer base to build on than loose or soft soil. You find loose or soft soil on an ancient lake bed or in a man-made landfill. During an earthquake, the waves go through loose soil as if the soil was liquid rather than solid. The waves grow larger and rock buildings like a giant ocean wave. Rocks do not make the waves larger, so buildings do not shake as much.

Windows

Windows for rigid buildings should not be too large. Tempered glass or a layer of shatter-resistant film can keep the glass from breaking into dangerous small pieces. Symmetrical windows help provide strength.

Flexible Buildings

Tall buildings must behave like trees bending in the wind. They must move as one unit. Floors should all be the same height and strength.

Reinforced Buildings

Metal straps, braces and other strengthening parts are used to help withstand the forces of an earthquake.

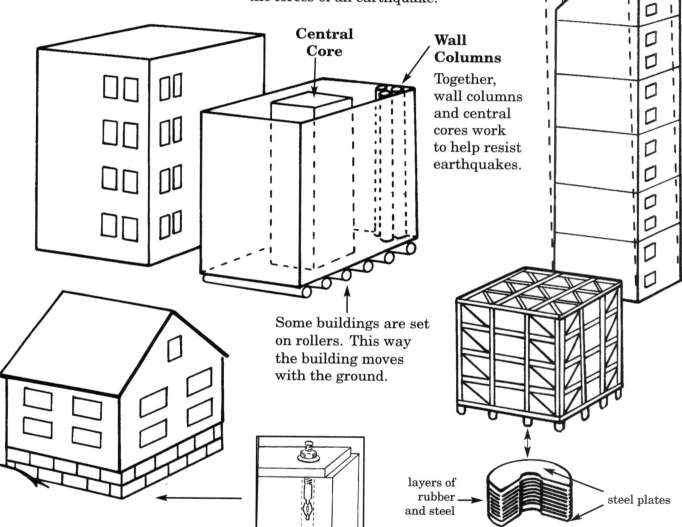

Central Core

Wall Columns

Together, wall columns and central cores work to help resist earthquakes.

Some buildings are set on rollers. This way the building moves with the ground.

layers of rubber and steel →

steel plates

Some buildings are set on **shock absorber**s or **isolators**. They separate the building from the ground. In an earthquake, the building should not shake as much as the ground.

Foundation

The foundation supports structures. It sits on or under the ground at the bottom of homes and buildings. It moves back and forth and up and down during an earthquake. It is important for the foundation to be bolted properly to buildings and homes. If it is not, then the buildings can slide or fall off of the foundation.

Be an Engineer

Engineers design new ways and materials to improve earthquake safety for buildings, bridges and homes. You can try to design a safe building, too. You will need popsicle sticks, toothpicks, cereal boxes, cards, sugar cubes, bullion cubes or other material. In the space above, **design some buildings to withstand earthquakes**. **Make your buildings**.

Test your buildings to see if they are earth quake proof. You will need something to imitate the soil or rock. For example, you could use a pan of Jell-O® and pretend it is loose, soft soil. Put your buildings on the Jell-O® and shake the pan a little, then more, then a lot. Or, put your buildings on a box to imitate harder soil. Make an earthquake by tapping the box with the end of a pencil or stick.

Shake Tables

In some labs, scientists use shake tables to imitate earthquakes. Japan has a **shake table** that is large enough to test a full-size building.

What should you do...

Check off one or more things you should do in each situation. Look up correct answers on the answer page.

...during an earthquake?

At Home

A. _____ stand by window

B. _____ stand away from shelves

C. _____ go under table, desk or bed

D. _____ run outside quickly

In Store or Building

E. _____ call home

F. _____ run for nearest exit

G. _____ go under a table or counter, tucking head down with both hands on back of neck

H. _____ use the elevator

At School

I. _____ go under desk

J. _____ scream and yell

K. _____ run to playground

L. _____ stand under the door frame

Outside

M. _____ stay outside

N. _____ go into nearest building

O. _____ stay away from utility poles

In Car or Other Vehicles

Q. _____ get out as soon as you feel shaking

R. _____ pull over to side of road when safe

S. _____ stay away from bridges and utility poles

T. _____ stay inside until shaking stops

...immediately after?

U. _____ call friends right away

V. _____ turn off gas and electricity only if the lines are broken

W _____ use phones only to report emergencies

X. _____ turn on battery powered radio for information and instruction

Y. _____ check for injuries and give first aid

Z. _____ use a fire extinguisher to put out small fires

...later?

AA. _____ go sightseeing so you can look at the damage

BB. _____ be prepared for aftershock

CC. _____ stay away from beaches and waterfronts

DD. _____ relax, the earthquake is over

EE. _____ go inside damaged buildings if they haven't fallen

How Long Do Earthquakes Last?

Earthquakes do not last very long. The **duration**, or length of time of the quake, may be less than 10 seconds or up to several minutes. It varies from time to time and place to place. Two minutes is a very long earthquake.

For all your incorrect guesses, you may want to talk with an adult about the correct things to do in an earthquake.

Answers on last page

Disastrous Outcomes

Earthquakes can do much harm to cities and people. Damage comes in many forms. Below are pictured several disasters. **Draw a line matching each disaster to a result**. **Then match the result to a place where this has happened.** See the key on the next page. You might find more than one answer.

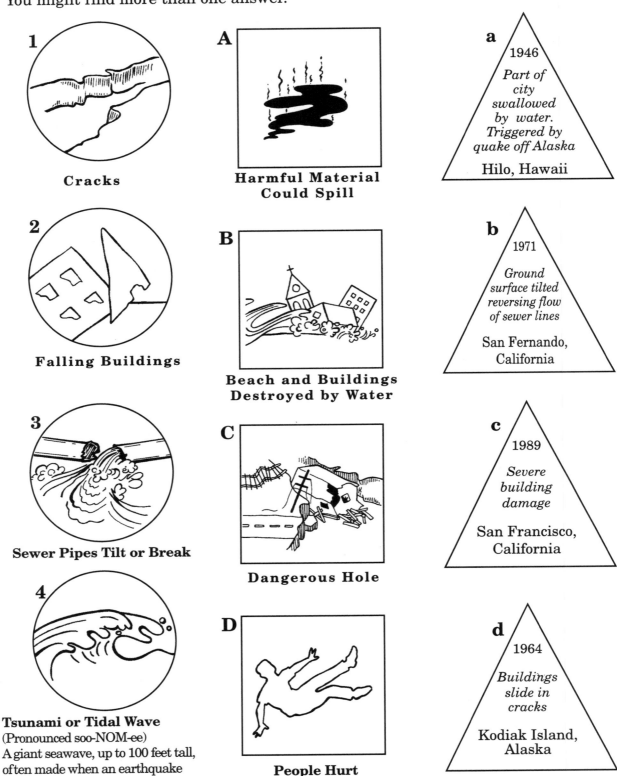

1 Cracks

2 Falling Buildings

3 Sewer Pipes Tilt or Break

4 Tsunami or Tidal Wave
(Pronounced soo-NOM-ee)
A giant seawave, up to 100 feet tall, often made when an earthquake starts under the ocean.

A Harmful Material Could Spill

B Beach and Buildings Destroyed by Water

C Dangerous Hole

D People Hurt

a 1946
Part of city swallowed by water. Triggered by quake off Alaska
Hilo, Hawaii

b 1971
Ground surface tilted reversing flow of sewer lines
San Fernando, California

c 1989
Severe building damage
San Francisco, California

d 1964
Buildings slide in cracks
Kodiak Island, Alaska

28

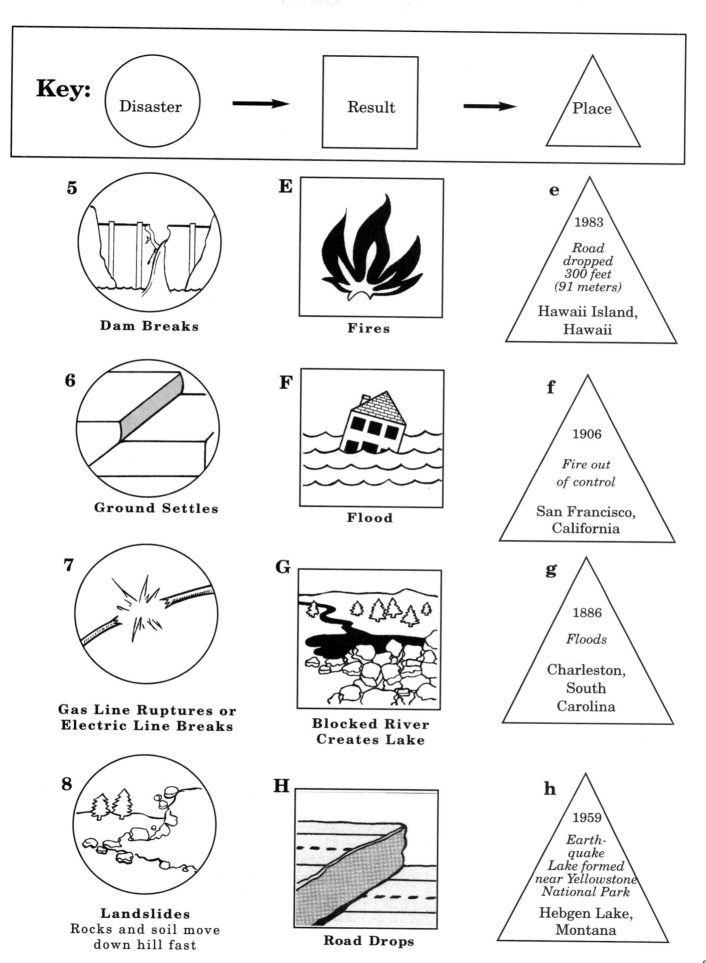

Key:

Disaster → Result → Place

5 Dam Breaks

6 Ground Settles

7 Gas Line Ruptures or Electric Line Breaks

8 Landslides
Rocks and soil move down hill fast

E Fires

F Flood

G Blocked River Creates Lake

H Road Drops

e 1983
Road dropped 300 feet (91 meters)
Hawaii Island, Hawaii

f 1906
Fire out of control
San Francisco, California

g 1886
Floods
Charleston, South Carolina

h 1959
Earth-quake Lake formed near Yellowstone National Park
Hebgen Lake, Montana

Globehopping

As a young seismologist, you have been given the job of visiting earthquake sites around the earth and reporting back what you learn. Travel this world maze and visit all the sites without retracing your own path. At each site, there is a symbol. Find the same symbol alongside the maze. Learn about some of the greatest and most interesting earthquakes that have occurred in the world.

 1556 China The largest number of people - 830,000 - ever to die in an earthquake.

 1959 Hebgen Lake, Montana, USA (near Yellowstone National Park) Landslide dammed the Madison River and created a new lake called Earthquake Lake.

START →

 1811 New Madrid, Missouri, USA The Mississippi River flowed ***backwards*** for a short time. Church bells rang as far away as Virginia.

 1906 San Francisco, California, USA Fires destroyed much of the city. 700 died.

 1964 Southeast Alaska, USA Tsunami and landslides created much damage. 131 died.

 1988 Armenia Buildings collapsed killing 45,000 people.

 1755 Lisbon, Portugal 70,000 killed - many in collapsing churches.

 1970 Peru Many landslides. 66,000 die.

 1985 Mexico City, Mexico A few hundred buildings collapsed as if they were on a bowl full of gelatin. 9000 died.

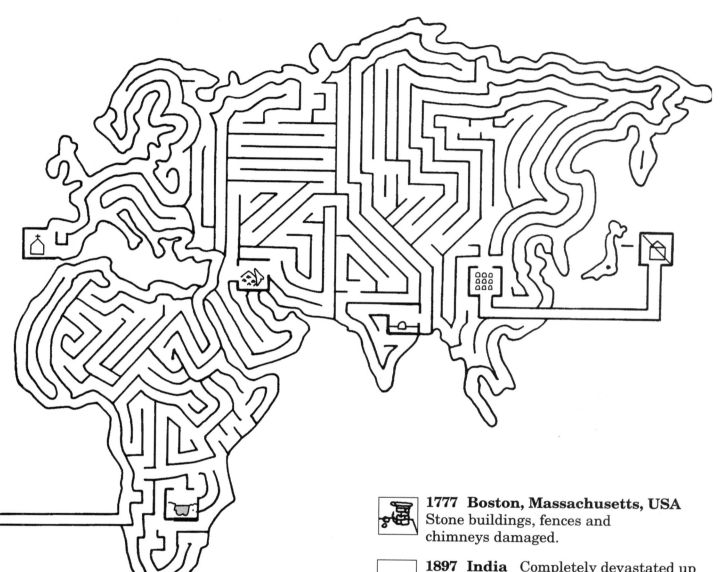

 1777 Boston, Massachusetts, USA
Stone buildings, fences and chimneys damaged.

 1897 India   Completely devastated up to 9000 square miles. Deaths were low because few lived here then.

 1923 Tokyo, Japan
1 million people left homeless 150,000 died.
1995 Kobe, Japan
250,000 left homeless 5000 died.

1958 Zambia   Over a 5 year period, water filled up area behind a new dam and caused 2000 tremors up to 5.8 on Richter Scale.

 1886 Charleston, South Carolina USA   Numerous mini craters, up to 20 feet wide, formed from sinking of loosely packed soil. 60 died.

 1960 Chile The largest earthquake ever recorded was 8.5 to 8.7 on the Richter Scale. 5700 died.

 1975 Hawaii, USA
Earthquake associated with volcanoes.

Mystery of Peaceful Cove

People have lived along the shores of Peaceful Cove for years and years. Although some of the grandparents remember dishes rattling, no one recalls an earthquake big enough to shake down houses. But then some clues in their backyards got the neighbors wondering whether Peaceful Cove might not always be so peaceful after all. Neighbors have started an argument. Be an earthquake detective and help solve the mystery.

Read the clues and examine the picture. Has there ever been a superquake here? Could there be one again?

Local Neighbor

I've lived here all my 89 years. Once or twice I've felt the ground shake. Back in 1949 an earthquake broke my best dishes. But our house didn't fall down, and I'll bet it'll still be standing when my grandson turns 89.

This isn't California. It is not earthquake country. Why do you think they call it Peaceful Cove? There aren't really big earthquakes.

Geologist

My Grandma is probably right, as usual, but she needs to remember that 89 years isn't very long for Mother Earth.

As a geologist, I try to figure out the Earth's history, which is billions of years long. We should look at least a few thousand years into the Earth's past before deciding whether a big earthquake can happen here.

A big earthquake could lift that beach so high that the waters of Peaceful Cove could never reach it again. A big quake could also cause that hillside to slide into the cove. We need to look for signs that changes like these have happened during the past few thousand years.

Archaeologist

My Grandfather told me a story from his Grandfather from the days before white people began to live here. Our people were dragging canoes onto the village beach where you and I swim in the summer. Suddenly the ground shook so hard the people could not stand. From across the water came a big cloud of dust. A landslide had splashed into Peaceful Cove. Soon a big wave was bearing down on the village. Many of the people saved their lives by running up the hill. The wave dumped sand in the buildings. I don't always believe these old stories, but I think this one may be true because last summer I saw a sand layer in an archaeological dig at the site of the ancient village.

Clues like these were found in the Puget Sound area of Washington state. However, the clues weren't all in one location. Scientists had to do clever detective work. Clues led geologists to conclude that a big earthquake occurred about 1000 years ago along a fault that passes beneath what is now downtown Seattle. During this earthquake, land along the fault rose about 6 meters (20 feet). A large wave was created in Puget Sound, and forests slid to the floor of nearby Lake Washington.

Peaceful Cove Before Earthquake

Can We Predict Earthquakes?

Just as you used clues to solve the "Mystery of Peaceful Cove," scientists use clues to try to predict future earthquakes. Predicting where, when, and how big an earthquake will be might prevent some damage and help save lives. Yet predicting quakes is very difficult.

There is an experimental earthquake prediction center in Parkfield, California. Scientists from several groups, including the United States Geological Survey (USGS), have placed different kinds of sensitive instruments around the area. The instruments help find, or detect, slight changes in the earth that might come before these earth-shattering events.

Some Changes Scientists Look For

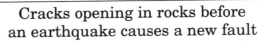

A slip along a fault before an earthquake

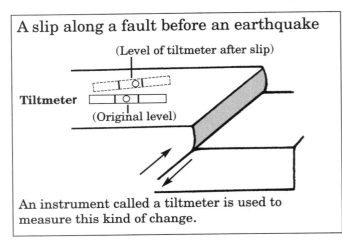

An instrument called a tiltmeter is used to measure this kind of change.

Cracks opening in rocks before an earthquake causes a new fault

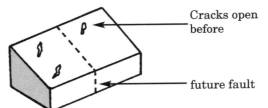

Escaping gas from rocks, presence of radon gas in water, or changes in well water levels might be used to measure this kind of change.

Two blocks of earth slipping relative to each other

If Block 1 slips in a different direction from Block 2, then the distance between two points will be longer. Compare Line A and Line B in the pictures below. Which is longer?

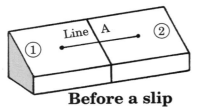

Before a slip

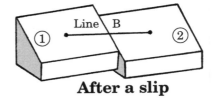

After a slip

A laser beam might be used to measure this change.

Answer on last page

Other complicated instruments measure changes too. When scientists think an earthquake may happen, they send a warning over the radio, television, and newspapers. A short-term prediction means that an earthquake is more likely to happen within a particular time period, for example, two days or three weeks. It does not mean that a quake is certain to happen. A warning may be canceled if the scientists get new information.

Every earthquake region in the world is different. The changes in the earth at Parkfield may be different from ones observed elsewhere. Whatever is learned at Parkfield will have to be tested in other earthquake areas before scientists can make predictions.

Strange Animal Behavior

"Do animals act strange before earthquakes?"

"Like people, animals are jumpy and no doubt act weird if they feel vibrations of foreshocks."

People report:

Horses rear and stampede.

Cows refuse to go into barns. Chickens won't go into coops.

Fish and shrimp come out of water.

Mice and rats come out in the open. Swarms of screaming seabirds appear.

Pandas moan.

In 1975, snakes in China came out of hibernation in February. This odd behavior, along with many foreshocks, did help save the lives of many people.

But most of these reports come a long time after the earthquake, sometimes up to two years later.

"Can animals predict earthquakes? No one can be sure at this time."

"Scientists don't have enough evidence. More scientific studies need to be done."

35

Can Earthquakes Happen

Most people don't think of eastern North America as likely earthquake country. Yet earthquakes do happen there. These quakes are harder to understand because they do not occur along faults we can identify at the surface. They are not as predictable as those in the west.

Color the large arrows number 1 red. They show the North American plate being pushed west and southwest by magma coming up from the Mid-Atlantic Ridge in the ocean. The North American plate doesn't move along smoothly. It builds up stress. It is a different kind of stress than is found along the west coast. Pushing by forces marked 1 squeezes or compresses the plate, causing **compressional stresses** to build up.

Color small arrows blue. These arrows show how this compressional stress is oriented in North America. Even though eastern quakes are generally smaller in magnitude, their shock waves are spread over larger areas. (See below.)

The stress is everywhere throughout the plate. The earthquakes may be occurring in the weaker parts of the plate.

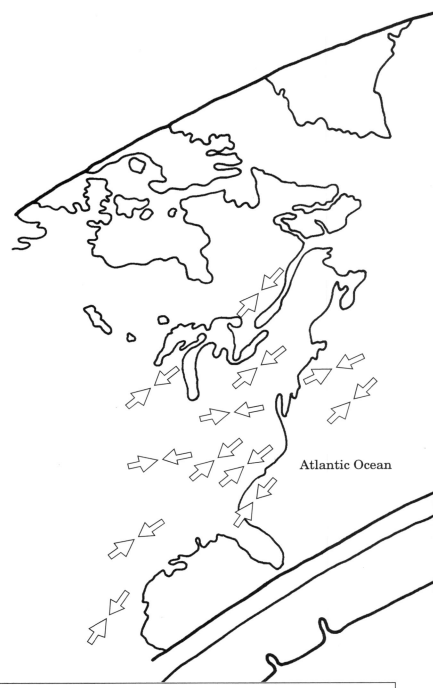

Atlantic Ocean

Why are these earthquakes felt so far away?

San Francisco, 1906 (Intensity VI or VII)

Spread of shock waves in the West

Underlying rock is colder and harder or stiffer in the east than rock in the west, so shock waves travel further. Also, the east is not covered by as much fault-shattered rock, which tends to dampen the spread of shock waves.

New Madrid 1811 (Intensity VI or VII)

Spread of shock waves in the East. Twenty times the area

in the Midwest or East?

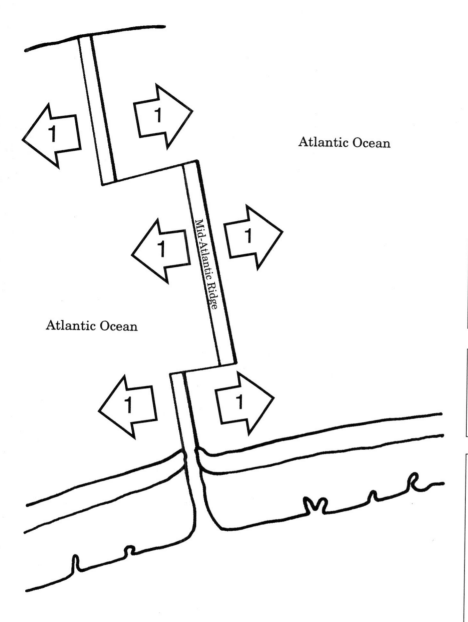

Atlantic Ocean

Mid-Atlantic Ridge

Atlantic Ocean

Draw an arrow from each box to the correct place on the map.

Newfoundland, Canada
A large quake in 1929 set off an underwater landslide which caused a tsunami or tidal wave that killed 27 people on the beach and broke an underwater telegraph cable.

Quebec, Canada
Over the last 330 years there have been five moderately large earthquakes.

New York, USA
Several faults underlie the area. A small quake was felt in 1985.

New Madrid, Missouri
Three strong earthquakes happened in 1811 and 1812. They were felt in Canada and Washington, D.C. Church bells rang in Boston. There was a noise like thunder. The bed of the Mississippi River was uplifted, causing the river to flow backwards for several hours.

Charleston, South Carolina
An earthquake damaged almost the entire city of Charleston in 1886. Dams failed, flooding nearby areas. About 110 people died. It was felt from Massachusetts to Wisconsin to the Bermuda Islands in the Atlantic Ocean.

Midwest States and Provinces
Earthquakes in the Midwest are rare. Little damage occurs. Small earthquakes, such as the tiny quake near Lansing, Michigan late in 1994, occur every few years. They might be due to the buildup of stress along old faults buried 100's to 1000's of feet beneath the surface. Earthquakes are uncommon in areas that are far from plate boundaries, like the Midwest.

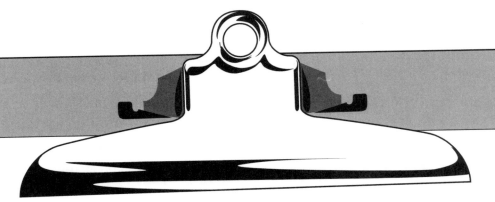

My Earthquake Plan

Fill out, copy and give to all family members.

Family Earthquake Plan

Emergency Meeting Place _____

(Outside your home)

Meeting Place _____ Phone_____

(Outside your neighborhood)

Address _____

_____

Family contact _____

Phone (____)_____ Phone (____)_____

day   evening

For US information write to: FEMA, P. O. Box 2012, Jessup, MD 20794-2012 or phone 1-800-280-2520

In Canada write: Emergency Preparedness Canada, 122 Bank St., 2nd Floor, Jackson Bldg., Ottawa, Ontario K1A OW6 or phone (613) 991-7077

Crossing
Quake Country

Across:

1. Waves which travel through the earth the fastest and are the first to reach the seismograph.

3. Spot or source of the earthquake within the earth.

4. The earth's crust consists of many _____ that move.

6. Scientist who studies earthquakes.

12. Sudden shaking, trembling, rolling, or shock of the earth's surface.

13. When plates of the earth move apart, scientists say they _____ .

14. The theory of plate _____ explains how the plates of the earth move.

15. Place on the earth's surface directly above the focus.

Down:

1. Everyone should be _____ and have an earthquake plan.

2. Smaller shake that follows the main earthquake.

3. Crack in the earth's crust where movement has occurred.

5. Giant seawave caused when an earthquake starts under or near the ocean.

7. A scale which uses Roman numerals to describe the damage caused by quakes.

8. A scale which uses numbers to represent the total amount of energy released by an earthquake.

9. When plates of the earth move toward each other or collide, they _____ .

10. The process of an ocean plate meeting and pushing under a land plate.

11. Scientist who studies the earth and what it is made of.

Answers

p. 5   A Long Time Ago: 1–D, 2–C, 3–B, 4–E, 5–A, 6–G, 7–I, 8–F, 9–H, 10–J

p. 6   Solving the Mystery: To guess what is in the package, you might look at the shape of the package and shake it. You would pay attention to the weight of the object inside, listen for any noise or sounds, or even smell the package.

p. 10   All Cracked Up: A. North American. B. Juan de Fuca. C. Pacific. D. Antarctic. E. Cocos. F. Nazca. G. Caribbean. H. South American. I. Scotia. J. Hellenic. K. Eurasian. L. Turkish. M. Arabian. N. Philippine. O. Indian. P. African. Q. Australian.

p. 13   Plates on the Move: It will take approximately 11,088,000 or 11 million years for Los Angeles to move next to San Francisco. (350 miles x 5280 feet per mile x 12 inches per foot = 22176000 inches /2 = 11,088,000)

p. 15   Stretch and Snap: The pattern in the pan would look like this:

p. 18 and 19 How Big Was It? A-II, B-III, C-I, D-IV, E-VII, F-VIII, G-V, H-VI, I-XI, J-IX, K-XII, L-X. On the pyramid line 4 is 27,000, line 5 is 810,000, line 6 is 24,300,000, line 7 is 729,000,000, line 8 is 21,870,000,000 and line 9 is 656,100,000,000

p. 20   Safe or Unsafe? The bottom room is the safer room. 1. The bed is away from window. 2. A lamp on the table is attached by velcro. It replaces the hanging lamp. 3. The book case is not attached to the wall with metal brackets and has guard rails to keep the books in place. 4. The cabinet above bookcase is now latched. 5. The high shelf on the wall now has a guard rail to keep the objects on the shelf. 6. The T.V. is built into a low cabinet instead of on a T.V. cart with wheels. 7. The hook holding up the hanging plant is now closed.

p. 27   What should you do? You should have checked off the following things to do in the different situations: B, C, G, I, M, O, R, S, T, V, W, X, Y, Z, BB, CC

p. 28   Disastrous Outcomes: 1-C-d; 2-D-c; 3-A-b; 4-B-a; 5-F-g; 6-H-e; 7-E-g; 8-G-h

p. 39 Crossword

p. 32   Mystery of Peaceful Cove: Yes, it is likely a super earthquake happened about 1000 years ago. The buried trees in the lake are from a landslide caused by an earthquake. The oysters were uplifted during the quake and now are exposed by a stream running through the area. Radiocarbon dating shows the buried trees and twigs in beach sand are over 1000 years old. The earthquake caused a tsumani which carried sand way up the shore and buried the buildings of the archaeologist's ancestors. This kind of evidence tells scientists an earthquake happened here before and could again in Peaceful Cove.

p. 34 Can We Predict Earthquakes? Line B is 1/8 inch longer than Line A.

Dog-Eared Publications thanks
seismologist Mary Lou Zoback (woman scientist illustrated in this book)
for assistance on *Discovering Earthquakes* and geologist Brian Atwater, for assistance
with the "Peaceful Cove" activity. Both scientists are with the U. S. Geological Survey.